ADVERTISING

SUSAN WAKE

MEDIA STORY

GEC GARRETT EDUCATIONAL CORPORATION

MEDIA STORY

ADVERTISING

BOOKS

COMICS AND MAGAZINES

MOVIES

PLAYS

TV AND VIDEO

Edited by Rebecca Stefoff

Cover: One of the many advertisements used by
the Coca-Cola Company.

© 1990 by Garrett Educational Corporation
First published in the United States in 1990 by
Garrett Educational Corporation
130 East 13th Street, Ada, OK 74820

First published in 1990 by
Wayland (Publishers) Ltd, England
© 1990 Wayland (Publishers) Ltd, England

Printed in Italy
Bound in USA

Library of Congress Cataloging in Publication Data
Wake, Susan
Advertising / Susan Wake.
p.   cm. — (Media story)
Includes index.
Summary: Examines the purposes, methods, and forms of advertising, and shows readers how they can make their own
advertisements
ISBN 0-944483-95-X
1. Advertising — Juvenile literature. 2. Television advertising — Juvenile literature.
[1. Advertising.]   I. Title.   II. Series.
HF5829.W35 1990
659.1 — dc20
90-3895
CIP
AC

CONTENTS

WHAT IS ADVERTISING?

ADVERTISEMENTS ARE all around us every day, although we are not always aware of them. We see ads on huge posters and in the middle of our favorite television programs. We hear them on the radio and flick through them in our magazines; but what exactly are they?

This beautiful poster is advertising a Japanese circus that is appearing in Madrid, Spain. Does it make you want to go?

Advertisements are "messages" paid for by those who send them to inform or **influence** the people who receive them. They come in very many forms and use many different methods to try to sell things to us. They also play an important part in telling us about things — for example, about health education. Advertisements remind us how to cross the road safely, or how to avoid the risk of accidents with fire. During election time we see posters and receive leaflets telling us about the different political parties and trying to influence the way we will vote.

Advertisers use a variety of **media**, including television, radio, posters, newspapers, magazines, or even the

More people go to the movies in India than anywhere else in the world. Advertisements for films appear in almost every Indian street, and lots of companies advertise in theaters.

sides of hot-air balloons. In different parts of the world some media are more important than others. In India, for example, far more people go to the movies than watch television, so the cinema screen is the most important area of advertising there.

Nowadays, advertising has developed into a very big business, as large companies compete for advertising time and space.

MARKETS AND TARGETS

ADVERTISING COSTS money. The media sell their space or time to advertisers. Producing advertisements is the work of highly skilled people who must be paid for their time. All this money and effort will be wasted unless the advertiser's message reaches the people for whom it is intended.

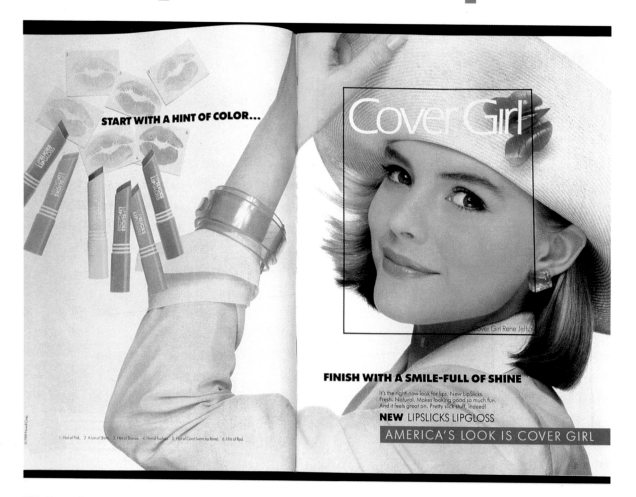

This advertisement for Cover Girl makeup appeared in a magazine for teenage girls.

Pepsi has used pop stars such as Michael Jackson (shown here) and Tina Turner to advertise its cola.

Every television and radio program, every magazine and newspaper has a profile. This is a rough idea of the kind of people who watch, listen to, or read it. People are grouped according to their **income**, lifestyle, sex, race, age, and so on. This means that advertisers can choose the programs, magazines, and newspapers that are most suitable for the particular product they are trying to sell. Finding out information about possible buyers is called market research.

Advertisers must also use market research to actually find the people most likely to buy, or who might possibly be persuaded to buy, their product. They must then target all their efforts at those people, rather than wasting time and money on people who are highly unlikely to buy anyway. For example, it would be no good advertising storm windows in a magazine for teenagers.

Advertisers design their advertisements to appeal to particular groups. For example, the advertisements for Levis 501 jeans are aimed at young people and try to make them feel that to be "hip and trendy" they must buy 501s.

Advertisers use many **techniques** that appeal to people's **emotions**. An issue in people's minds at the moment is the environment. People are concerned that the products they buy should be healthy and not harmful to the environment. Such so-called "green issues" have become part of the long list of methods used by advertising agencies to persuade us to buy.

A good example of this is the phrase "no additives or preservatives" on the labels of many foods. It has appeared on many items that never contained "additives or preservatives" in the first place. Advertisers, however, feel that

This advertisement for Kelloggs Crunchy Nut Cornflakes claims that the product has extra vitamins and iron. This is meant to make people think that Cornflakes are healthy.

more people will buy these items with this new label.

Often the availability (where it can be bought easily) of a product decides where and how it should be advertised. Local businesses would do best to advertise in local newspapers or on local television stations. On the other hand, an oil company could advertise in the national press and on national television because its product is sold all over the world.

Taken all together, the media make it possible for the advertiser to reach the whole population or any part of it, from large groups to small ones. One of the skills that goes into successful advertising is finding the right "mix" for the advertiser's purpose. This is the job of the advertising agency.

ABOVE Ads in a Tokyo street

BELOW The Conoco oil company uses former football hero Terry Bradshaw in a lot of its advertising.

9

A CLOSE LOOK AT ADVERTISING

TAKE A close look at a selection of advertisements in magazines and on television, particularly ads for your own age group. Now try to answer these questions for each advertisement.

1. What type of person will be reading the magazine or watching this program?
2. Who is the particular advertisement aimed at?
3. How is it meant to make the viewer or reader feel?

Which age-group do you think this advertisement for Converse All Star Boots is aimed at?

Colorful neon advertisements light up a night-time street in downtown Hong Kong.

4. What are the good points about it?
5. What are the bad points about it?
6. Do you think it is successful?

Look at a list of programs on **commercial** television for one day. Divide them up roughly into these time slots.

> 8 am – 12 noon
> 12 noon – 4 pm
> 4 pm – 6 pm
> 6 pm – 9 pm
> 9 pm – >

What might you expect to find advertised during these particular times? You must first decide who is most likely to be watching television at certain times and what the advertisers feel they might be able to persuade them to buy.

If possible draw up a chart that shows:

1. Who you think might be watching.
2. What you think might be advertised.
3. What was actually advertised (only during the programs you are allowed to watch).
4. You might ask an adult to do the same for the late night programs.

If you are able to do this a few times you should find yourself learning more about advertising techniques and being able to guess more accurately the types of advertisements likely to be shown at particular times of the day.

THE PEOPLE INVOLVED

IF YOU were to advertise your bicycle for sale in the window of a local shop, there would be three people involved: you, the shopkeeper, and the buyer. It is similar in the advertising industry.
There are:

1. The advertiser — this is the producer of the goods who spends money to advertise (like you, if the shopkeeper charged you a fee).
2. The media — the people who own and control newspapers, magazines, poster sites, and television and radio channels (like the shopkeeper).
3. The **consumer** — the person who buys the goods advertised (like the person who buys your bicycle).

Advertising agencies are used by most companies to produce exciting advertisements.

AME CALINE

LE ROI DES FOURMIS

LE BAL DES LAZE

LA MICHETONNEUSE

One of the best poster sites for advertisements is a public transportation stop.

In the advertising industry there is a fourth role, the advertising agency. This is a company that makes its money by producing advertisements for other companies.

There are so many different ways to advertise, so many different media to use, and so many people to reach that getting the best out of advertising is a highly skilled job. Advertising is a very **competitive** business. Many agencies all try their best to get contracts from the many wealthy companies with goods and services to be advertised.

What the agency does

A company may wish to increase the sales of an existing product that has not been selling well recently. The company has to decide how many items it would like to sell. This is called the sales target. It must also decide how much it can afford to pay for advertising. This is called the budget. Having done this, the company then asks a number of advertising agencies for ideas on how to reach the target. When the agencies have come up with some ideas, the company chooses the one that suits it best. This agency then takes a good look at the product it is to advertise.

Agencies are divided into different departments. The Research Department will find out about the annual (yearly) sales of similar products and compare them, to tell the company its **market**

Two art directors from an advertising agency. They are responsible for choosing the storyboard.

share. It will also carry out market research on large numbers of people, asking such questions as:
1. Have you ever seen this product?
2. Have you ever bought this product?
3. When did you last buy it?
4. If you stopped buying it, why?
The Research Department also needs to know the type of people buying and not buying — for example, their age, sex, and job — so that it can aim the advertising at the right people.

The people in the Creative Department will organize an advertising plan, called a campaign, and present a storyboard of their ideas to the company. A storyboard is a cartoon-like strip showing different ideas for the advertisement.

The Media Department will suggest the most suitable media. In selling your bicycle you had to decide where to advertise, how long to advertise, and what the costs would be. It would have been no use taking space in a national newspaper where the cost would be more than the bicycle was worth!

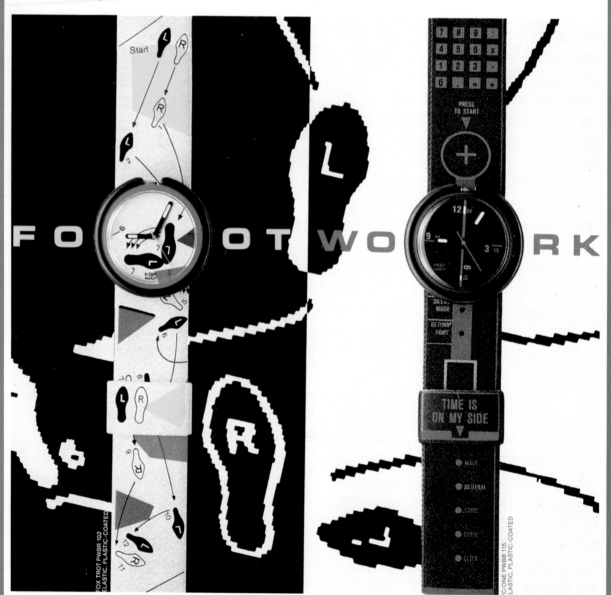

The Creative Department designs the advertisements, and the Media Department decides which magazines or newspapers should contain the ads, such as this one for Swatch.

When the company has looked at all these ideas and perhaps made a few alterations, it will give the **go-ahead** and production of the advertisement will begin. The agency begins the process of taking its ideas from a piece of paper into a finished advertisement. Many people will be involved in this process. They will work as a team. The Creative Department will find artists for magazines, newspapers, and posters, and scriptwriters and producers for television and radio advertisements.

For a television advertisement alone, the following people are usually involved:

> the producer
> the director
> the assistant director
> actors
> announcers
> camera crew
> lighting crew
> sound crew
> wardrobe expert
> makeup expert
> properties buyer
> set designers
> set builders
> musicians
> editors

The Media Department books suitable "slots" of time and space on television and radio, in magazines and newspapers. They will have worked out the best places and times for their

Many Brut products are advertised as being for "macho" men. They have used Sylvester Stallone, hero of the "Rocky" movies, to help create this macho image.

advertisements to appear, but there is great competition for these slots. Because of this, the costs are enormous.

Even after the advertising campaign has begun, people in the Research Department will still be working. They need to find out how people feel about the campaign. They also need to discover if sales have increased, and this information must be reported back to the company to decide if the campaign has worked or not.

TELEVISION

THE GREATEST advance in advertising came with the introduction of television. Advertisers could now reach into people's homes and tempt them with all kinds of things. Of course, as more and more homes got television sets, the number of possible buyers grew. Television was to become the most expensive, but most effective, way of advertising.

Benetton concentrates on color in its advertisements. This makes people think of very bright colors when they think of Benetton.

This is a very simple advertisement, but it manages to carry over the Benetton image of bright and original clothes.

Today millions of people watch television, so large companies spend huge amounts of money making television advertisements. These usually last less than a minute, but the tunes, **slogans**, and jingles can stick in our minds for years. However, advertisers cannot just advertise anything they want on television. They are strictly controlled by organizations that have been specially set up to make sure ads do not **offend** anyone. There is more information on this in the chapter on "Rules about Advertisements" on page 20.

Television advertising varies in different countries. In some countries, the advertisements are collected together in **batches** of up to ten minutes. In others, including the United States, advertisers are allowed to **sponsor** whole programs and to repeat their message as often as they wish. The limit for advertising time on British television is six minutes in any one hour. The viewer must be able to easily tell the programs from the advertisements.

The advertisements are sold as "spots" that can last from a few seconds to over a minute. The costs vary according to the size of the viewing audience. The more people likely to be watching, the more expensive the cost of an advertising spot. **Peak viewing times** are from 5:30 pm to 10:30 pm. Popular programs — major sporting events, for example — will have very

Andrex use Labrador puppies in their advertisements to make us think that Andrex toilet roll is soft and strong, like a puppy.

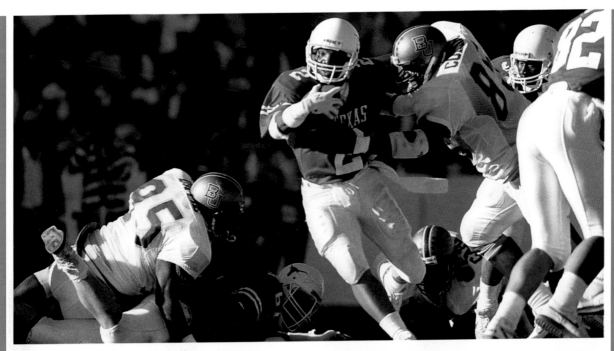

ABOVE Football is an extremely popular sport in the United States. Companies have to pay a lot of money to advertise during televised games.

RIGHT Athlete Grace Jackson is competing in an event sponsored by McVitie's cookies.

expensive spots during their broadcasts. For example, spots during a Super Bowl game can cost as much as $600,000 per minute.

Television broadcasts can be national (reaching the whole country) or regional (reaching particular areas of the country). Products for farmers, for example, would be better placed to reach country areas rather than towns and cities.

RULES ABOUT ADVERTISING

ALL COUNTRIES have rules about advertising. Some of these rules come from the advertising industry itself, to keep its good name, and others are enforced by law.

The rules about advertising in Canada are decided by the Canadian Advertising Foundation.

If advertisers were allowed to tell lies in their advertisements, people would eventually find out and probably not believe them next time. If an advertisement were to offend people, it would not work and would be a waste of both time and money. If an advertisement were against the law, it could result in a costly court case and loss of business. So it is in the advertisers' interests to keep within the rules.

The rules of advertising say how many advertisements can be used and where. For example, they say how many advertisements should appear in newspapers and the amount of time allowed on television for ads.

In the United States, the Advertising Review Board is the "rule book" for all advertisements, except those on television and radio. It says that all advertisements should be legal, decent, honest, and truthful. It says they should show responsibility to the consumers and to society. They should follow the business rules of fair competition. The Board is the "watchdog" of the advertising world. Its equal in Britain is the British Code of Advertising Practice.

The rules about advertising cover many things, but some of the areas with which they are most often concerned are:

Claims about price cuts
The use of well-known people

Many companies use sportspeople to advertise their name. Racing driver Saturo Nakajima is covered with logos.

Comparing similar products or services
Claims for medical products
Advertisements aimed at children
Cigarettes and alcohol
Dieting aids
Hair-care products

Certain products and services cannot be advertised on television at all. These include cigarettes, spirits (strong alcoholic drinks, such as whiskey or vodka), private gambling, and funeral services. Companies can often get around this by sponsoring certain events, particularly sporting events, where competitions and trophies bear the company name and are mentioned a lot in newspapers, on television, and on radio. At the events, huge boards bearing the company name and product names are in **prominent** positions to be seen by all in newspaper photographs or on television. It costs companies large amounts of money to sponsor such events, but this is often cheaper than buying advertising time and space in the normal way.

Most countries have an organization to receive complaints from viewers or readers about advertisements.

An Australian-rules football game. Companies often advertise at sports stadiums. They know that when the stadiums appear on television thousands of people watching the event will be able to see the advertisements.

There are strict rules about advertisements aimed at children. For example, all advertisements for phone services must tell children to get their parents' permission before dialing. Advertisements suggesting dangerous things are not allowed, but there are no rules to prevent television programs that are shown simply to sell certain products. Some cartoon series are offered free to

The television program "Thundercats" is really one long advertisement. It has helped to sell Thundercats books and dolls of the characters such as Lion-O.

Some companies make television programs about their products, such as Care Bears and Transformers, as a form of advertising.

television networks because of the money to be made on toys and other goods. Each time "Thundercats" and "Care Bears" are screened, they act as hidden advertising for products sold in stores.

Do advertising controls work? Because the controls are so strict, nearly all advertisements keep within the rules. A few slip through but are usually spotted by the public and reported to the organization that deals with complaints. Individuals may not like some advertisements, but the controls that govern advertising have nothing to do with personal taste. They are supposed to make sure that ads do not deceive the public, offend people, or break the law.

MAKING YOUR OWN ADVERTISEMENTS

IT CAN be good fun to design and organize an advertising campaign. It takes many people working as a team to do this, so you and your friends might like to divide into groups to make up your own advertising agency.

Look through some magazines to see how the advertisements have been designed.

Everyone will have particular skills that they can contribute, so try to organize the groups so that people can work in areas that they are good at, just as a real advertising agency would. For example, those who are especially good artists might like to work on the artwork for magazines and newspapers, and those who enjoy acting might like to be involved in the television group. Good musicians also play an important part in advertising.

Imagine that you are an advertising agency working for a company that is launching a new chocolate bar called GO. It is a chunky chocolate bar containing nuts and raisins, and the company that makes it would like it to have a healthy image of giving you energy to keep you going through the day.

1. The Market Research Group
This should be the first group to begin work. This group will need to do some market research to find out as much as they can about possible buyers and what they are looking for in a chocolate bar.

The market research group will need to design and use a **questionnaire**.

Some questions might be:
What is your age?
Are you male or female?
How do you select a bar of chocolate?
At what time of day do you usually eat chocolate?

If possible, use a computer to check the results of your market research.

Are you influenced by packaging (the wrapper or package)?
Is the price important?
It might be possible to use a computer to organize this information when it has been gathered.

When this information has been collected, the whole class will need to discuss the overall theme of the campaign. All the different media — television, radio, magazines, and newspapers — should be working together to repeat the same "message" in different ways. You will need to choose slogans and jingles that can be used throughout the campaign by all the groups.

2. The Television Group

Design a television advertisement for your chocolate bar. If you are fortunate you may be able to use a video recorder. Points to consider:

You only have 60 seconds for your advertising spot, so accurate timing is very important.

Whom is your advertisement aimed at? Be sure that the brand name is repeated often enough and that it can be seen clearly.

Don't forget that music may be important in your advertisement.

3. The Storyboard Group

This group will need to work closely with the television group to design different storyboards for the television commercial.

Design a television advertisement for the GO chocolate bar.

The radio group should use a tape recorder to record the jingle.

Points to consider:
Storyboards are made up of words and pictures. They can actually win or lose business for advertising agencies, so they must be exciting and colorful and must show exactly what is going to happen in detail.

4. The Radio Group
This group has to design a 60-second radio advertisement.
Points to consider:
Sound effects, music, and clear speech will be very important.
Use a tape recorder to make your advertisement.
Accurate timing is very important as you have exactly 60 seconds.

5. The Magazine and Newspaper Group
Design color and black and white

Which magazine would you place your advertisement in?

advertisements for magazines and newspapers.
Points to consider:
Size must be considered. Look in newspapers and magazines to get ideas. You will need to do rough sketches of ideas before deciding on the final advertisements.
Will the advertisements be the same for all types of magazines or will you need different ones for different age groups?
Clear lettering and eye-catching illustrations will be important.
It is important that you have regular meetings so that all groups can report back to the whole class on their progress and everyone has the opportunity to contribute ideas.

REMEMBER — Rules about advertising are strict. You cannot lie or make false claims.

QUESTIONS TO BE ASKED

Does advertising work?

ADVERTISING MUST work or advertisers would not continue to use it, because it can cost a great deal of money. The price of advertising space depends on the type of newspaper or magazine, the kind of people who read it, the number of copies sold, and the size and exact position of the advertisement.

Do you think this advertisement works?

The symbol of Ronald helps to sell McDonald's burgers.

The cost of advertising time on television or radio varies according to the size of audience that the station expects to have at the time when the advertisement goes out, and, of course, on the length of the ad. A big campaign using national newspapers, magazines, and television can cost enormous sums of money, but large or international companies that run this kind of campaign have sales running into hundreds of millions of dollars each year. Advertising represents only a small fraction of the total cost of producing, **distributing**, and selling their goods. It is possible, of course, to advertise more cheaply — on local television stations, for example.

Advertising must work, but it cannot work on its own. It cannot sell a product that is no good. It cannot make people change their views unless they are ready for their views to be changed. However, often people are unaware that their views are being shaped. Many of us might prefer not to be bombarded from all sides by advertisements.

Advertisers and agencies can check up on how effective their advertising is. When a product is being advertised they can look at the difference in sales before and after a campaign, to see if more items have been sold since the advertising began. They can use market research to discover people's reactions to the ads.

Who benefits from advertisements?

All of us who watch commercial television or listen to commercial radio stations and buy magazines or newspapers benefit because of the money made from advertising. If more goods are sold as a result of advertising, the maker's costs are reduced and this helps to keep prices down. So advertising can help the consumer.

What is the future of advertising?

Many things around us change rapidly. The **technology** exists to change the whole business of buying and selling goods and the advertising that goes with it. In the area of television alone, the introduction of remote control and video means that we can avoid advertisements if we wish. Satellite and cable television and teletext have opened up a whole new area. The growing number of home computers may mean that one day we will not have to leave home at all to shop. Perhaps we will just see the advertisements and press buttons, and goods will arrive.

Many people believe that advertising just creates a society that wants more and more; but there are some positive points too. Ads are needed to spread useful information, particularly in such areas as health education. Advertising can also be fun. But it is a big, powerful, and extremely wealthy industry, and we must remember that its target is us!

GLOSSARY

Batches — Sets or groups.

Commercial — Television stations that sell space for advertising.

Competitive — Involving rivalry and competition.

Consumers — Users, buyers.

Distributing — Delivering goods around the country.

Emotions — Feelings, of happiness, sadness, etc.

Go-ahead — Instructions to begin.

Income — The amount of money people earn.

Influence — Something that affects people.

Market share — The proportion of goods a company sells compared with its competitors.

Media — The different means of communication used by advertisers, such as television, radio, newspapers, magazines, posters, etc.

Offend — To hurt people or to displease them.

Peak viewing times — The times when the greatest number of people will be watching TV.

Prominent — Clearly seen, outstanding.

Questionnaire — A list of questions used to gather information.

Slogans — Short sayings used by advertisers to draw attention to their goods.

Sponsor — To put money into something in order to get advertising.

Techniques — Methods of doing things.

Technology — The science or study of manufacturing processes.

BOOKS TO READ

Communications by Keith Wicks
  (MacDonald, 1985)
Newspaper by Andrew Langley
  (Franklin Watts, 1985)
**The School on Madison Avenue:
  Advertising and What It
  Teaches** by Ann E. Weiss (E. P.
  Dutton, 1980)
**Marketing and Advertising
  Careers** by Marc Solomon and
  Norman Wiener (Franklin Watts,
  1977)

Index

The numbers in **bold** refer to captions.